I Am Fit!

by Carmel Reilly

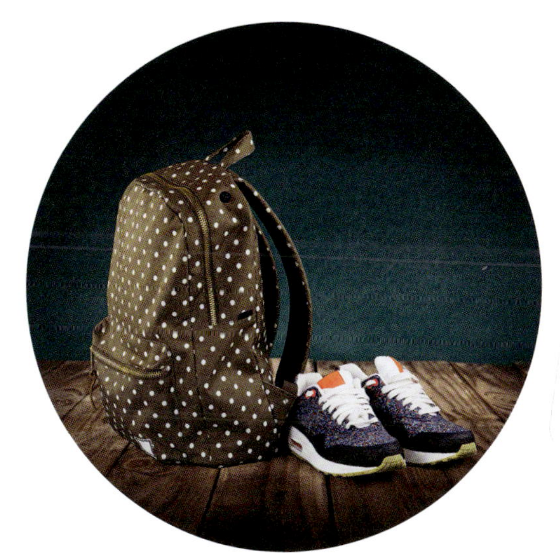

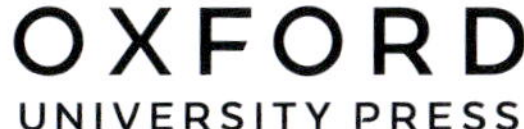

I get up.

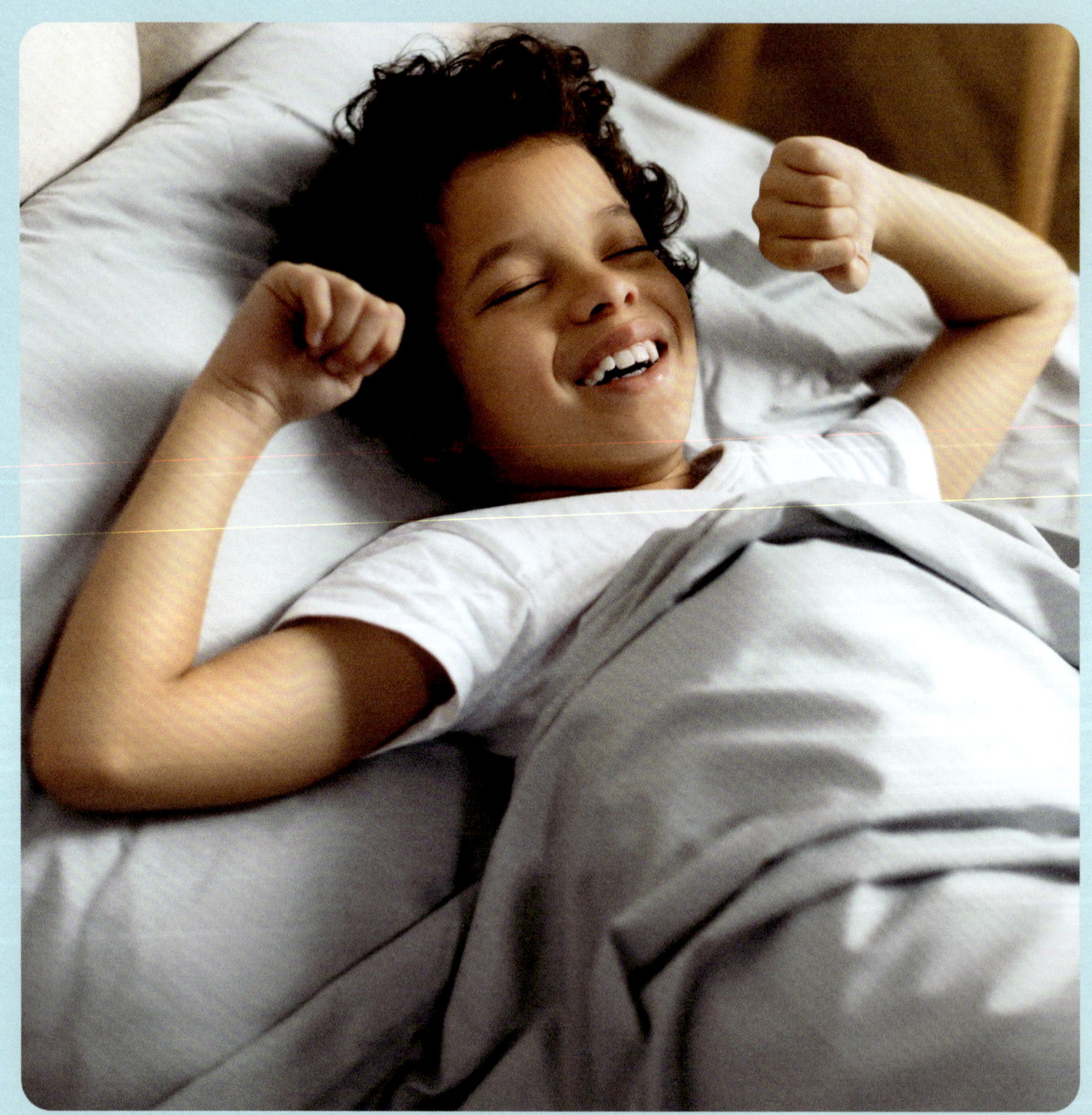

I put on a hat.

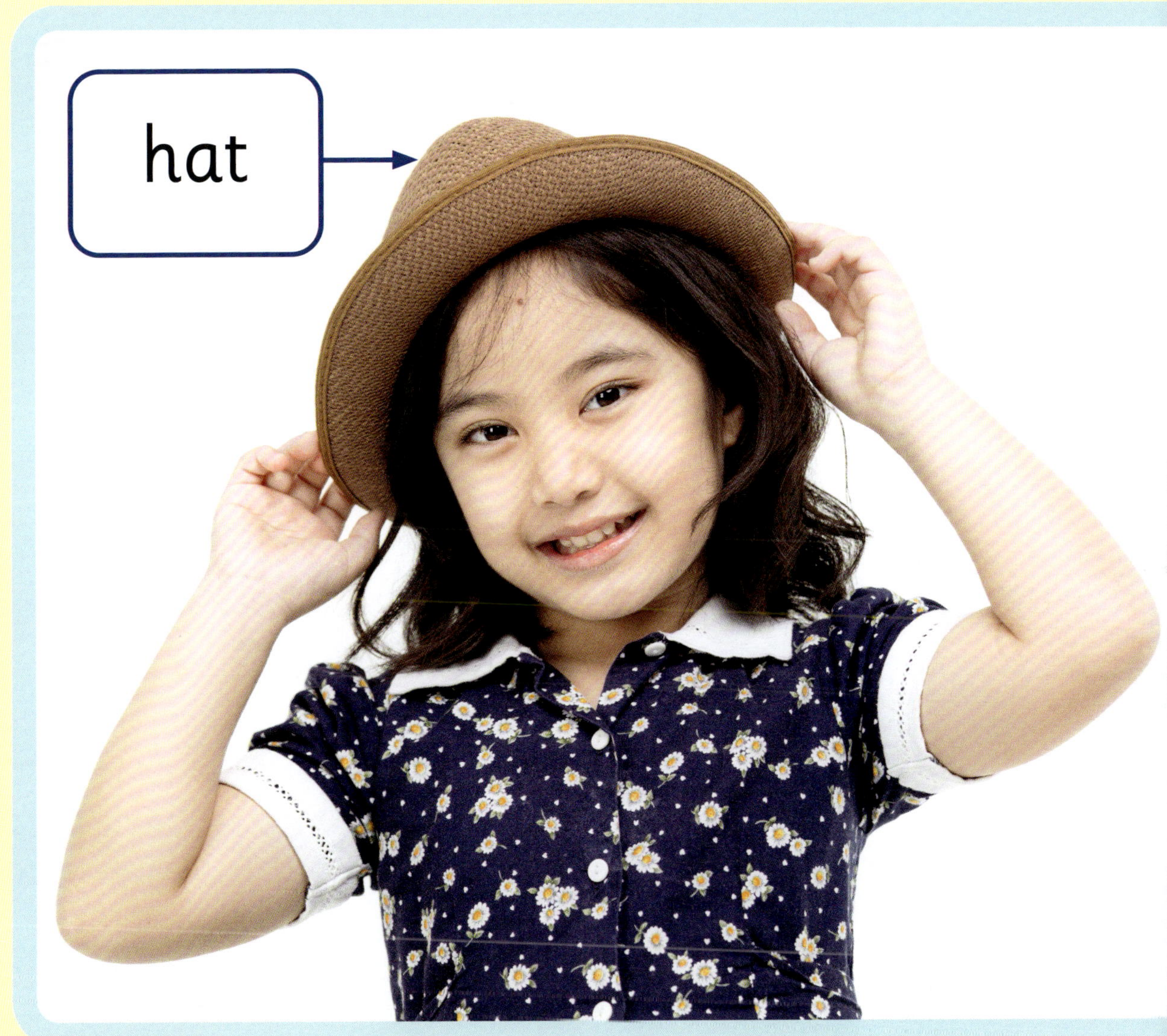

I run as Pop sets off.

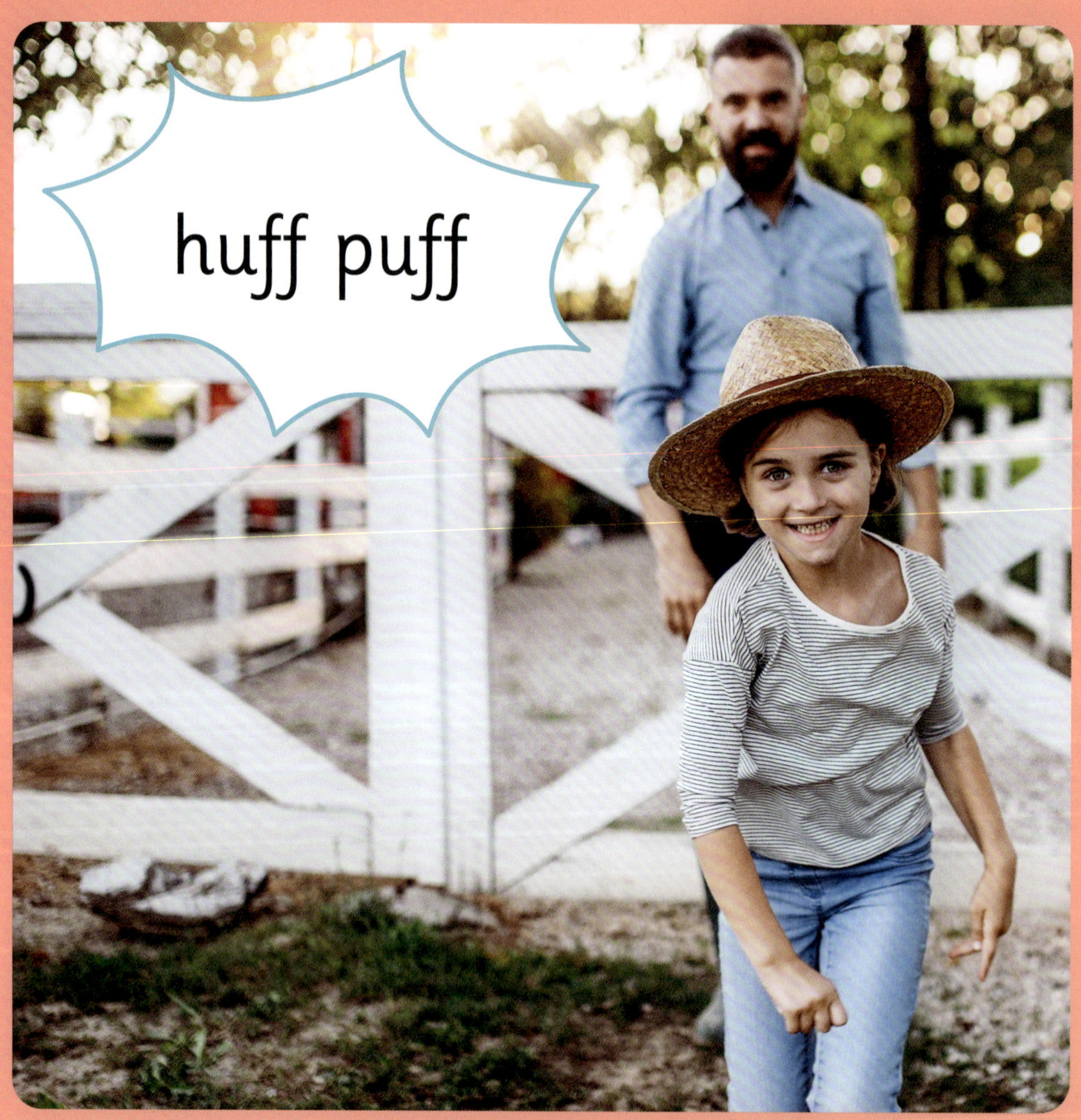

A run is fun.

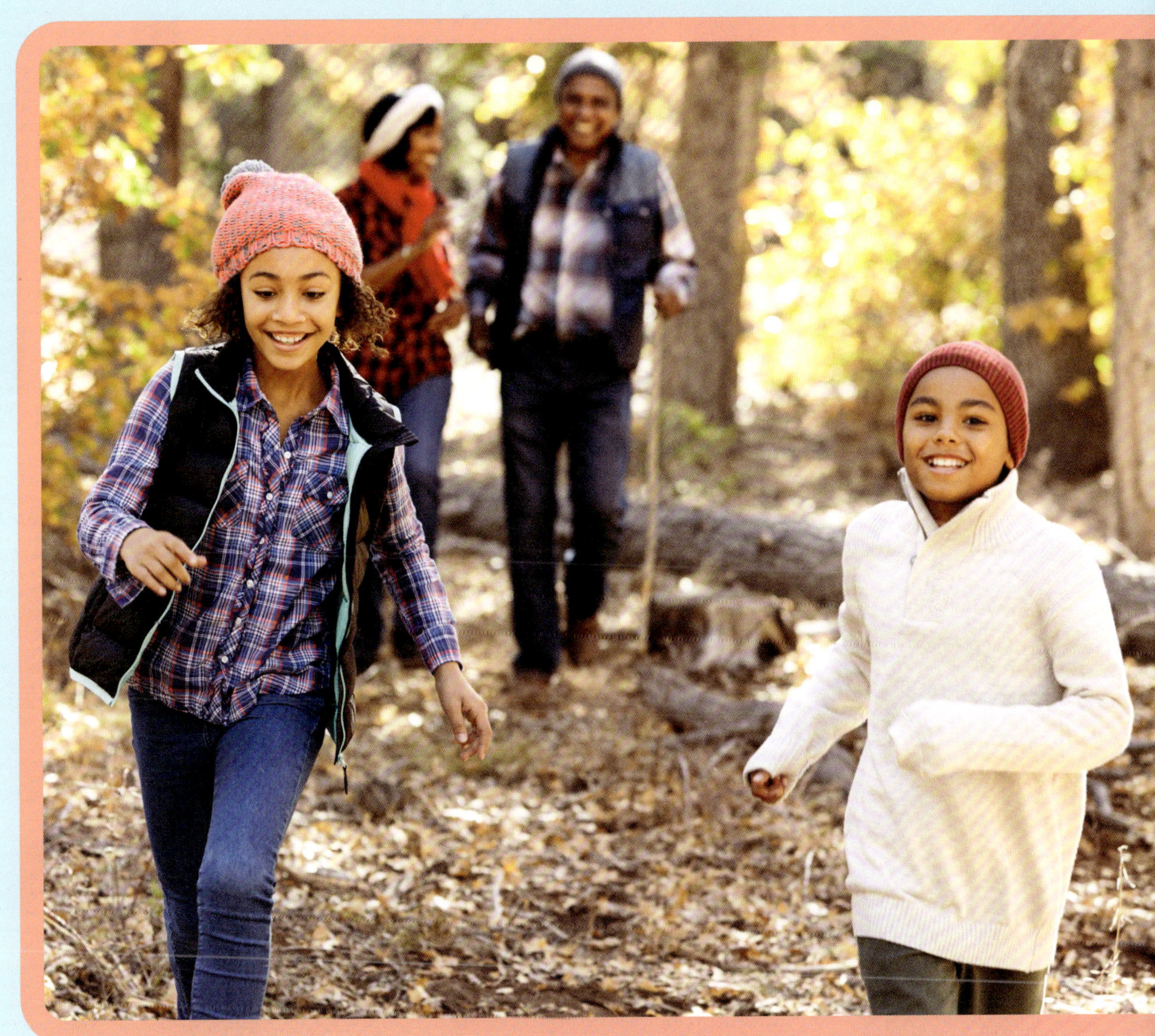

I hop on a log.

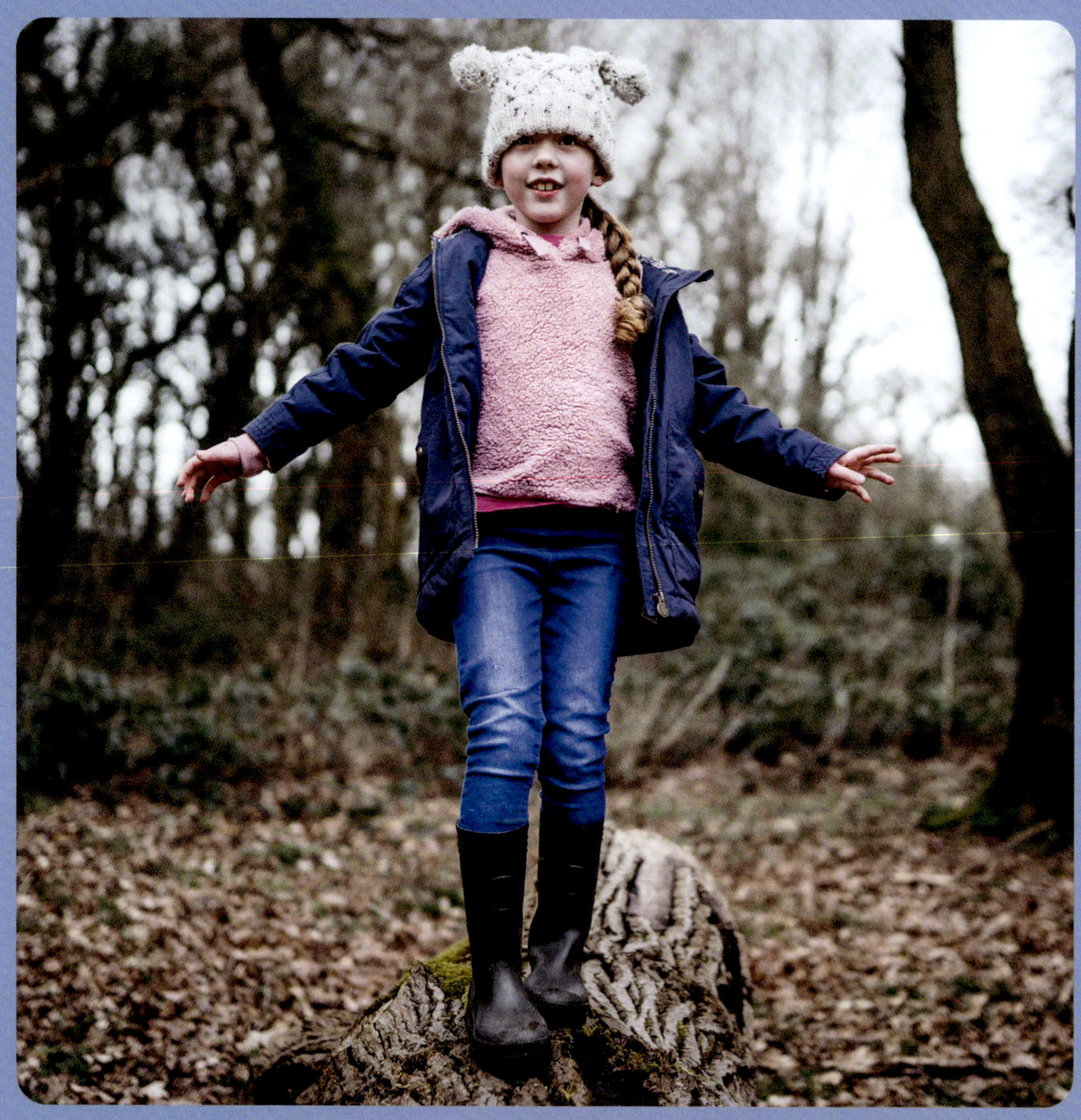

I get a bag.

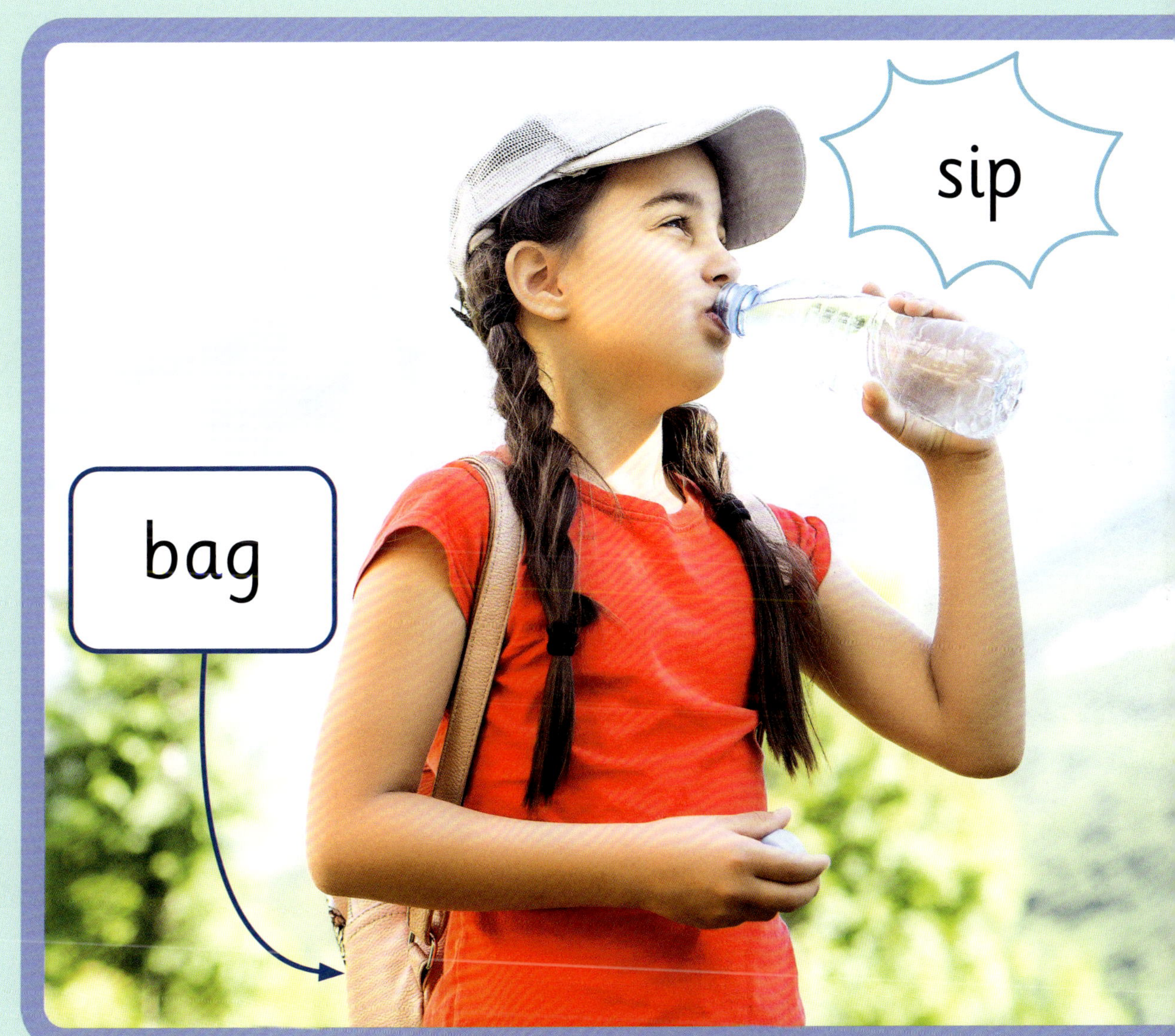

It is lots of fun.

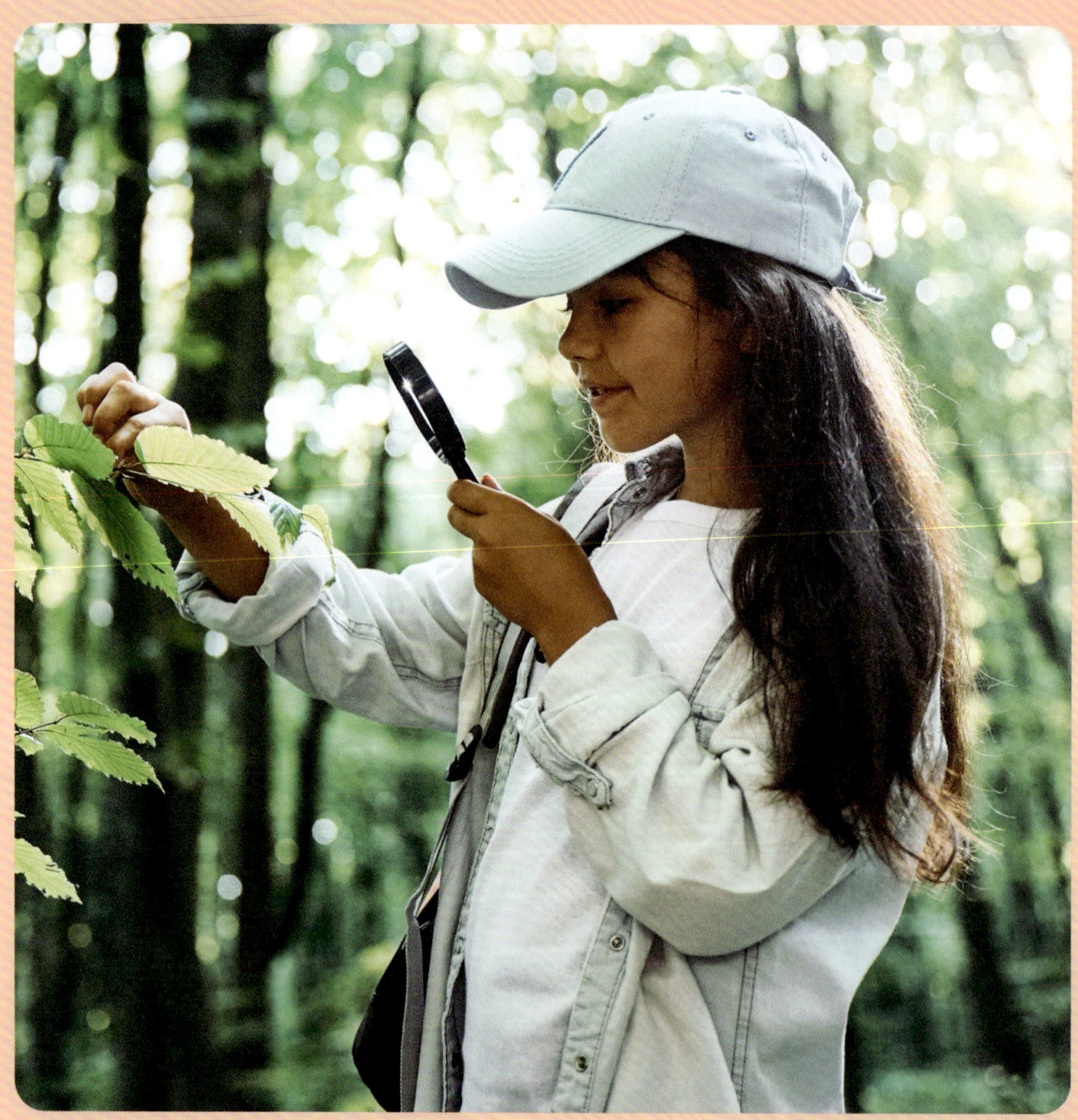

I can run back.

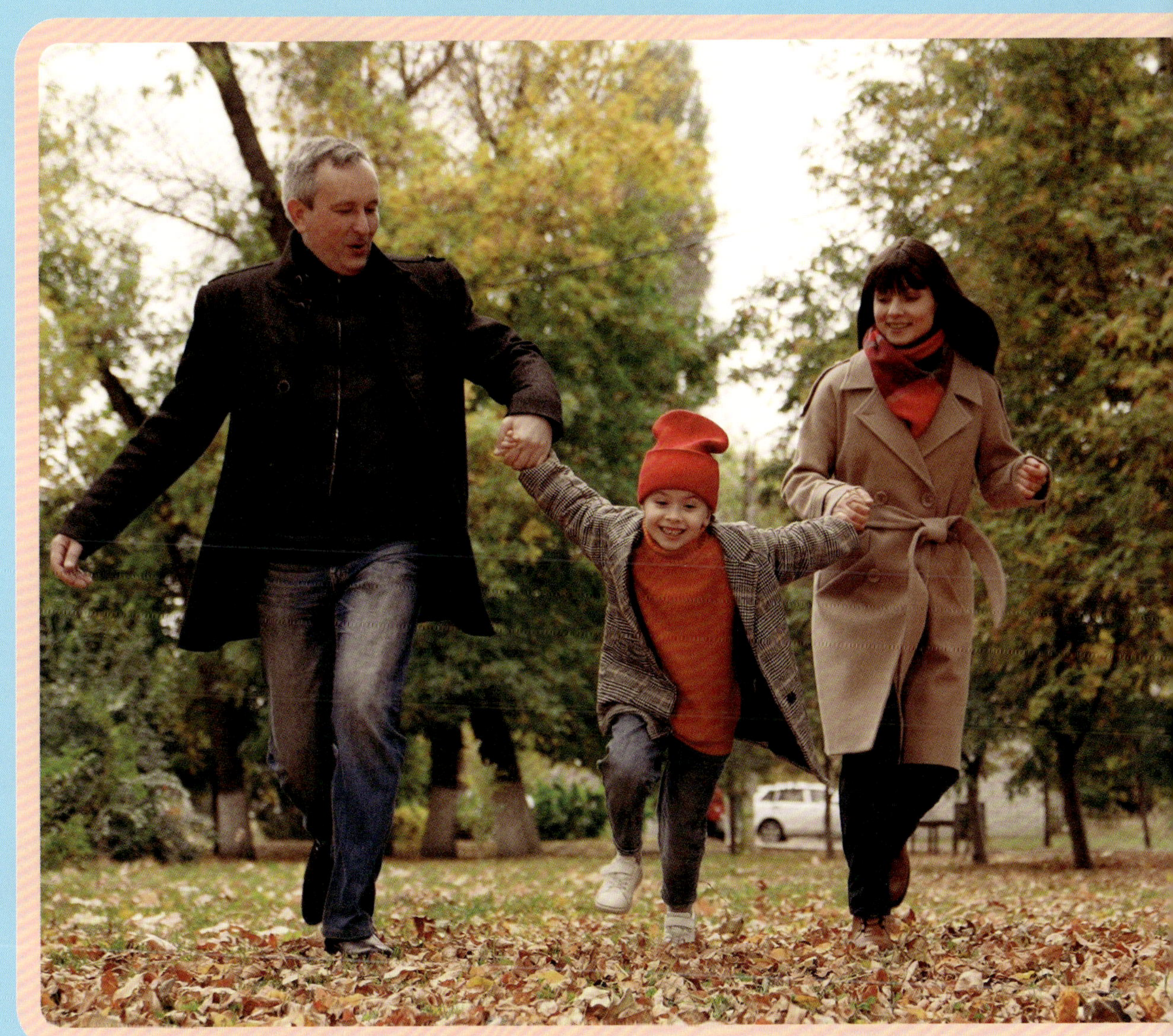

I can go and go.

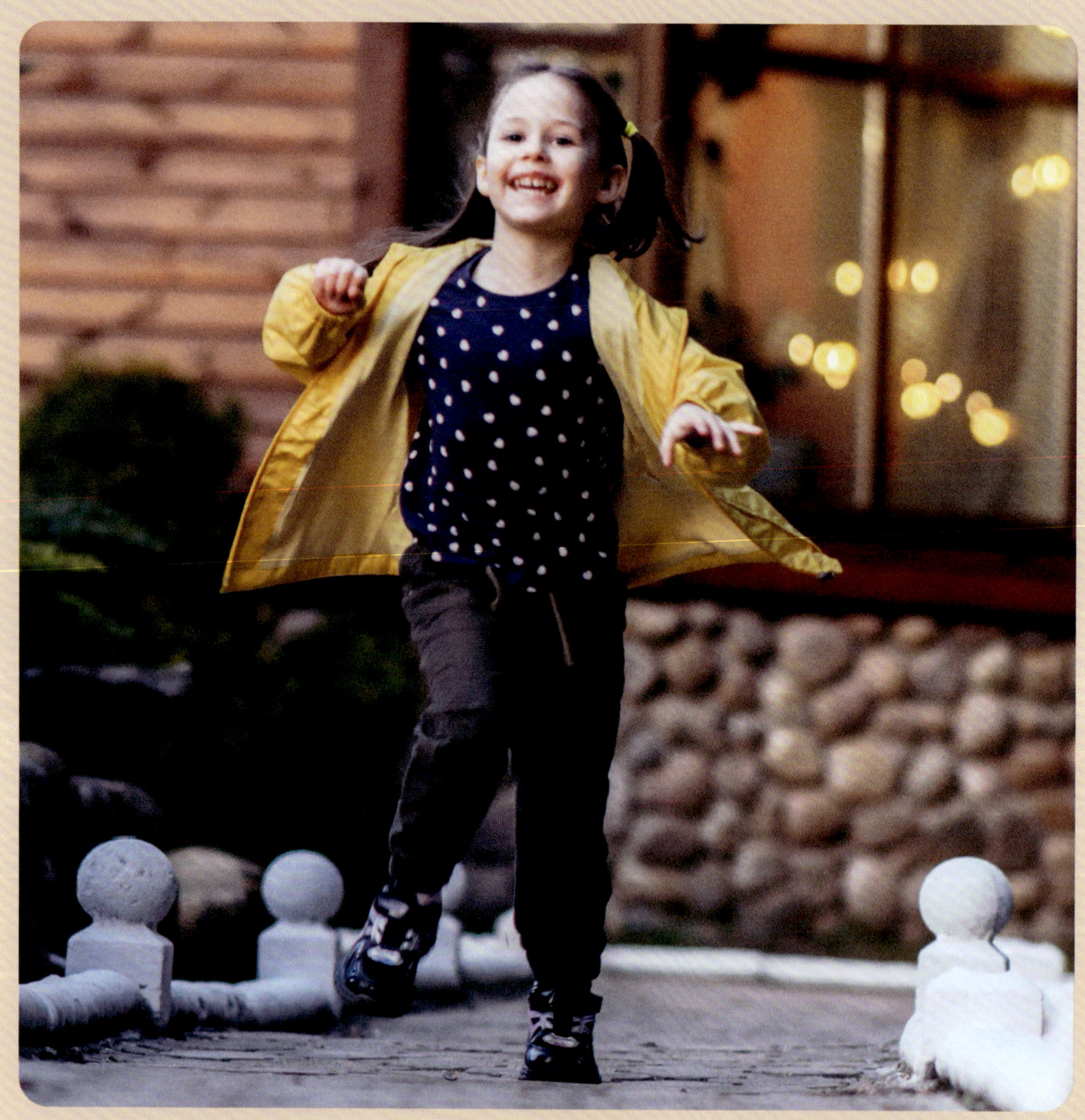

I am fit.

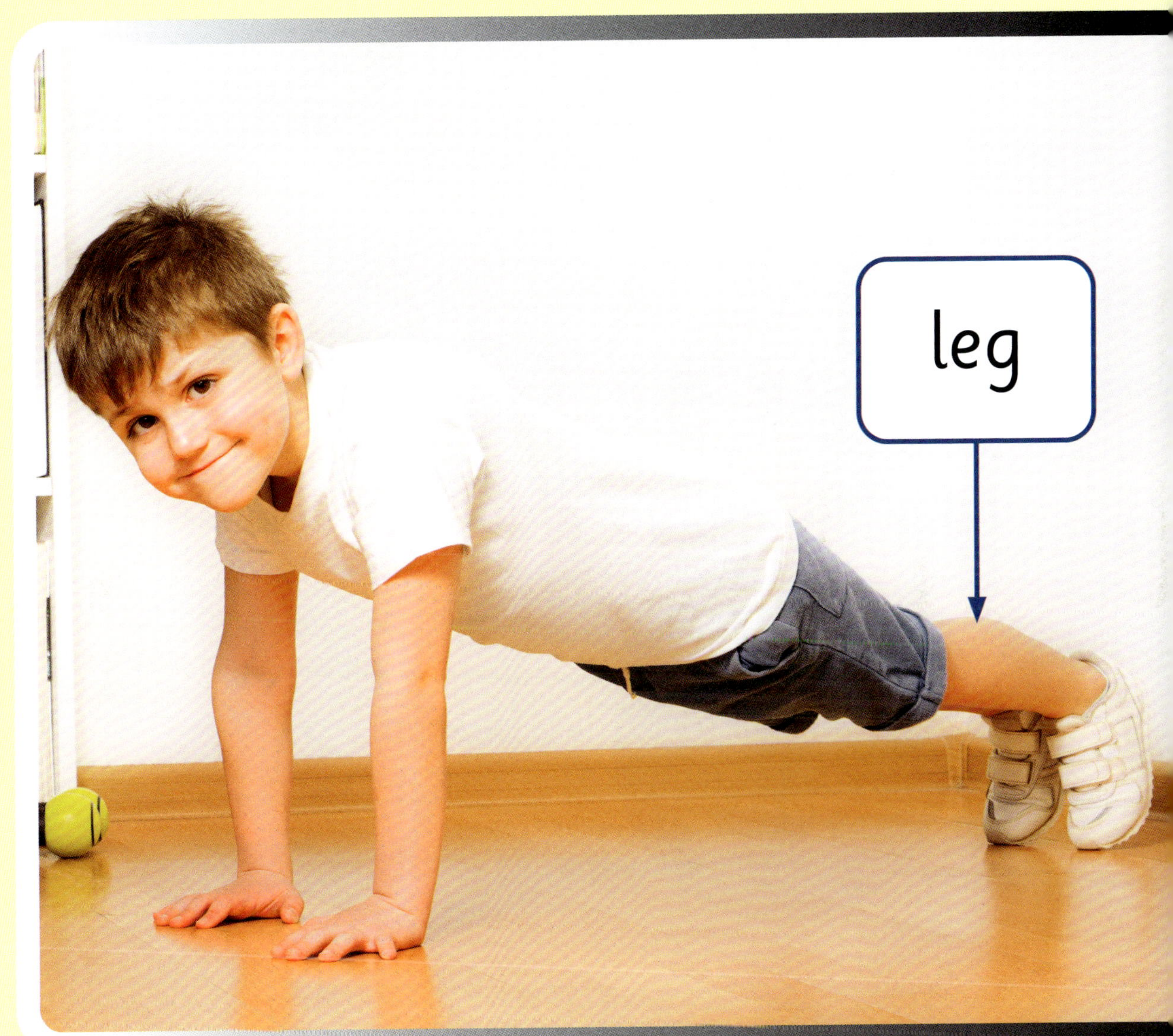

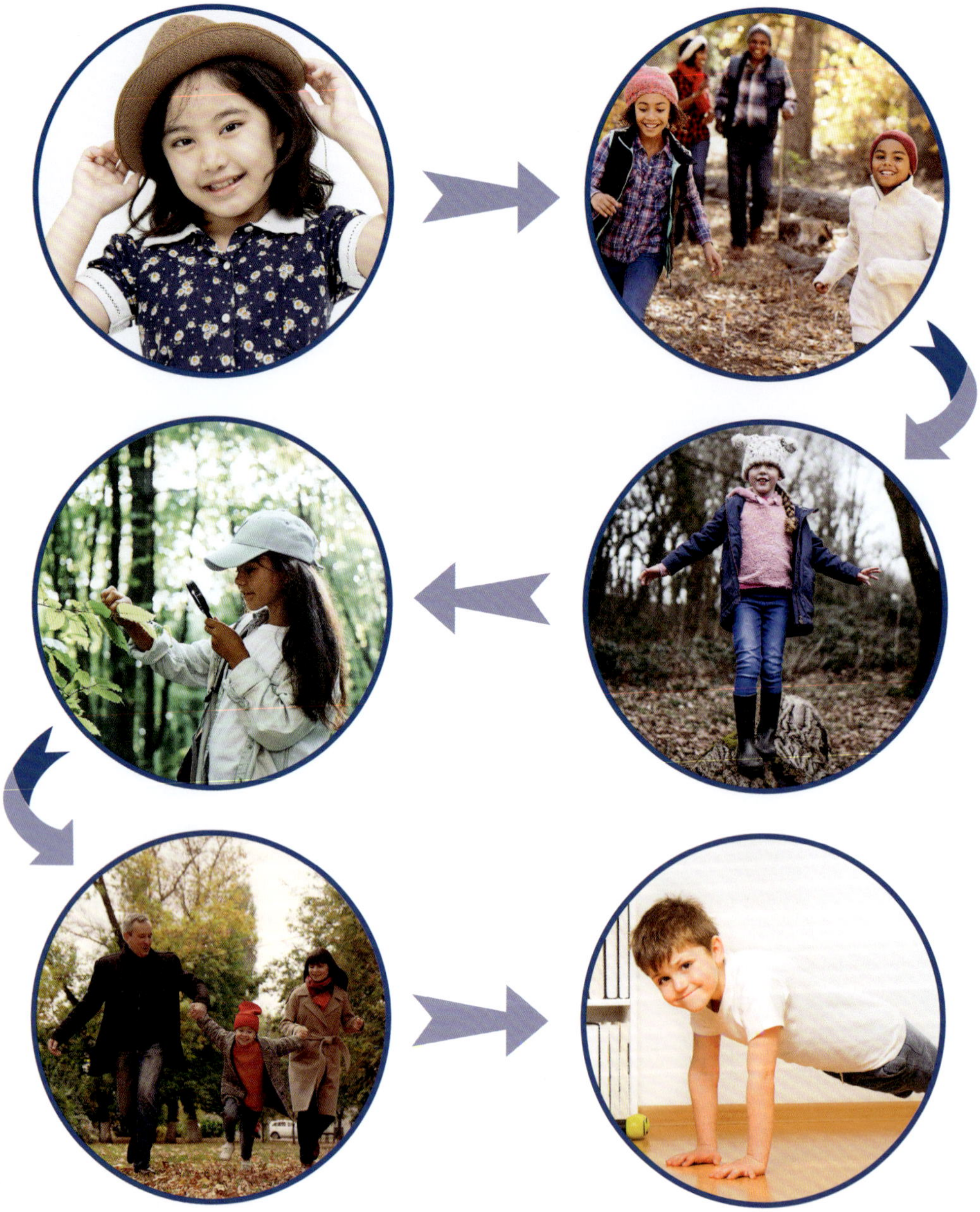

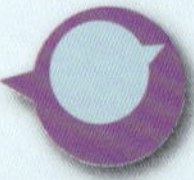

Encourage students to use the images to review the topic.